A R R I V A L   P R E S S

MESSAGES FROM THE HEART

Edited by

TIM SHARP

First published in Great Britain in 1997 by
ARRIVAL PRESS
1-2 Wainman Road, Woodston,
Peterborough, PE2 7BU
Telephone (01733) 230762

Copyright Contributors 1997

HB ISBN 1 85786 543 X
SB ISBN 1 85786 538 3

FOREWORD

The poems in this collection reflect the good times, the bad times, the fun and the sad times experienced through true love. The emotions expressed are powerful and come straight from the heart.

This anthology combines poems of first love, failed love and even poems from people searching for love, to create a truly inspirational read.

I hope you enjoy reading this collection of verse.

Tim Sharp
Editor

CONTENTS

LOVE ETERNAL

I care for you my love,
I care with all my heart,
I made my vow with God above
That we would never part.

I love you because you're gentle
I love you because you're kind,
And you are sentimental
With a caring, thoughtful mind.

I never want to change you,
I love you as you are,
Even through all eternity
Our love will shine afar.

Jean Lloyd-Williams

I CAN'T LET GO

You live on like memory.
In fact your loss has driven her out
My whole body belongs to you
A touch, an embrace, yet a kiss
I see your eyes
I pan your lips
My eyes the relationship's camera.
I couldn't figure this empty scene
I considered badness
but now I am here,
I don't know where to go.
I try to move forward
but your smile holds me back
Your hands stroke my body
and your eyes tell me to love you
So I do . . .
Deeply . . .
Insanely
and so passionately . . .

S Simms

HELPING HAND

Your heartache shows.
As you move you cup your heart,
Trying to keep hold of the pieces.

Let me hold them for you.

Nicola Brook

Something Deep Within

You said you would come
But then you were reluctant
You said you loved me
But how could you?

I gave you everything
You gave me something
Something deep within
But do I want it?

It hurts me
It burns deep down inside o' me
Do you know what it's like?
Do you feel the pain?
Do you feel the same?

Michelle James

FIRST LOVE

Time! It has no meaning, for two when in love,
'Tis manna to each, sent from above;
Holding each other or just side by side,
Eyes for each other - with no one to guide.
Hand in hand goes the young boy and girl,
Two hearts beating fast, two heads in a whirl;
The hands on the clock - they do not see,
How late it is getting, at home they should be.

How many young souls have felt the same?
Late getting home *first love* it was to blame;
To leave each other? They both vowed 'Oh no!'
But time passes on and separate ways they did go.
Now let this be a lesson what I say to you,
For this boy and girl this love wasn't true;
It happens so regular - most every day -
But true love when it happens, with each other you'll stay.

Leslie F Dukes

WHAT IS LOVE?

Love is such an unselfish thing,
It comes from inside,
     Deep down within,
Love comes in many different ways,
     But the feelings of love,
     You cannot part,
Because it comes straight,
     From the heart.

Jackie Boote

CONTINUED?

In love but afraid.
Happy but sad.
Excited but nervous.
Shocked but glad.

What do you do after all these years,
When you've finally met the man in all your dreams?
He comes along out of the blue,
Unexpected and really really cute.
You become very close after a month or two,
But then one night what does he do,
He goes off and doesn't return,
He's been with another lass and leaves you in pain.
He's always there in the back of your mind,
But you keep going and hold your head up high,
Years later you see him again,
You tell your friend that you really like him.
She goes over and points you out,
He doesn't like you without a doubt.
But then he smiles,
He glances your way,
What should I do? What should I say?
Should I go over or should I stay?

In love but afraid.
Happy but sad.
Excited but nervous.
Shocked but glad.

Catherine Robertshaw

TO MY HUSBAND

Why is it, as the anniversaries come and go,
You grow more dearer with the passing years,
My other half, my lover, husband, friend,
Who understands my yearnings and my fears.
While you are with me life is full and sweet,
Without you, I am lost and incomplete.
The thread of love that interwinds our lives
Grows ever stronger, and its ties
I never want to sever,
But stay within its wondrous spell forever.

Ethel Rayment

AFTERMATH

Hush my darling
The storm has now passed.
Stripping the past
Of all dead wood.
A scaffold constructed
Uplifting - our future to come.

To know your smile
Enter your secret thoughts.
That pain and tumult
Can never erase.

You hold my happiness
Safe from the hurricane
Of bitterness and recrimination.

Cleansed with my tears
Absolved.
Our future intact,
Hush my darling
The storm has now passed.

Sally-Ann Lawson

BRIEF ENCOUNTER

Love is knowing
He stands nearby,
Out of your sight
But inside your mind.

You taste him still
The forbidden fruit,
You touch with your eyes
But not with voice.

Who is this man
So near but so far,
My lover my friend
My other half.

To have this joy is heaven sent
It lasts not long,
But a moment in time.

The hours fly by
Now you are gone,
A rose I lay
on the cold, cold earth,
You sleep forever
I am still awake.

Elsa M Summers

LOVE!

Love what does it mean?
Is it the sparkle in your eyes
The brightness the sheen?

Is it the friendly hello
When you want so much more
Or is it the holding of a door?

You love someone with all your heart
Only to drift apart

Love is it worth all the pain and sorrow?

You think never again
Well maybe tomorrow!

They say you will know when the time
Is right
Was it the fumble in the darkness
One starry night?

Love will it ever happen to me?
Or should I leave it to destiny?

B Marston

TO YOUR LOVE

Thank you for love,
Love four letters filled with power,
L for light and laughter
O for the opportunity of knowing you
V for the very being of you for ever after
E for everything you are and do.
Love is learning about you
Every minute and hour.

Every day is a fresh new start
You gave your life for my very being
Always be in my mind and heart
You are the very universe,
All doing and all seeing.

June Witt

LOVE BY THE POUND

Why isn't love
Sold by the pound
In Tesco's
To be wrapped up
And carried away
In shopping bags?
If it were
I could buy
A pound or two
To give you as a gift
To store in the larder
Of your heart.
Perhaps you could
Put it in my tea
A spoonful at a time
To sweeten my life.

Frank Coldwell

DREAM OF YOU

Darkness fills the room, and I lay on the bed,
Reels of pictures, begin to fill my head.
Eyes are closed, but I still see,
All the things, that used to be.
Memories that are good, I decide to keep;

Only hurtful ones, are buried deep.
Freezing the frame, within my dream;

You are better there, than you've ever been.
Only I can make things come true,
Upon my bed, in a dream of you.

Deborah Wells

My Husband

Colin you're my husband whom I love with all my heart,
To me it is a special love I knew right from the start,
You're sensitive and caring in every single way.
Our bond I think gets stronger each and every day.
I love your smile you make me laugh,
And tease me when I'm being daft,
You sing me songs and lullabies,
And melt me with your sky blue eyes,
I really just can't resist them,
You're like a drug going through my system.
My feelings run like mountains high,
My love for you will never die,
I hope you feel the same way too,
As I whisper the words, 'I love you.'

Fiona McNab

ANGEL EYES

Darling darling angel eyes
In my verse there are no lies
This poem is written just for you
And every word is true
My love for you was so very strong
But I handled things all wrong
Now my life is like a long sad song
O you cannot know the pain
When I'm sure you view me with disdain
How I wish and wish you could look my way
And smile again for me one day
Because my love for you
Can never fade
Darling darling angel eyes

Marda

WHEN STARS COLLIDE

When stars collide, and planets die
I'll see your beauty and I'll sigh
From wishing that I was belonging
With you for whom my arms are longing

When you were born, the angels saw
No other soul as sweet as yours
When you illuminate the night
The jealous stars can't match your light

So every time you smile at me
My soul ascends to ecstasy
But you love him, you don't love me
So you won't kiss me tenderly

The treasures that the earth can yield
The gold and silver from a field
Or gems, translucent pure and true
Are not as wonderful as you

Philip McLynn

A TRIBUTE TO MY FRANK

He is a man who walks with God,
He's always caring and sharing,
His love of all people, Kathy and me,
His joy is of no ending,
He is a giver, but not a taker,
That's how he likes to be.
But I'm proud of my Frank,
Who gives so much,
But all of his devotion to me.

Rosetta K Smith

FROM ME TO YOU

Although you're not here, I express my love for you
Although it is wrong, I need you
Although I am here, you are not
Although love is hate, it is not

When I say I am yours, I am
When I give you my love, I damn
When I feel your heart, I see
When I feel your love, I be

I am in my heart, a flame of love
I am in all passion, a motion of doves
Fly to my soul, open your heart
Fly and be free, let go of the dark.

Nicola Buxton

ENIGMA

Cocooned walls, from which journeys begin,
Intricate thoughts, caress a hazy skin,
Misty thoughts, clear to radiant skies,
You creep slowly in, when I close my eyes.

Unreal, enigmatic, though I believe I see,
Intangible friend, I hear you calling to me,
Reaching in anticipation, alas out of reach,
Warm feels the sand, remote is this beach.

A million warm winds, cross this land,
Gently reaching out, you take my hand,
When your lips touch mine once more,
I am carried to that distant shore.

I blink and you have disappeared, again from reach,
Into the shimmering sand, covering this golden beach,
I close my eyes once more, and I see you beckon to me,
With undying love, we enter into the seas of eternity.

Mark McLean

THAT CERTAIN SMILE

That certain smile,
The bridge it crossed.
Towards new light,
But it got lost.
Tender is the night,
When dreams are played,
Within a mind,
Where tears once stayed.
Though they soon fled,
Frosty nights return.
Hope, still in good stead,
Tries valiantly to burn.
But love and sorrow,
I've seen you in force.
I try to fight you.
Failing of course.

Rachael Shipston

COULD LOVE BE

Could love be that stirring within, a mysterious and profound feeling,
That puts your heart and mind in a whirl, and sends your senses reeling,
Which makes the days grow shorter, forever probing your inner being,
Plummeting you into thoughts anew, with eyes that are closed,
                                                        yet seeing.

Could love be a mother's caring for her children, when times are bad,
Surmounting the snares and turmoils of life, when all seems very sad,
Protecting with her very life, when peril and danger appear again,
Prepared to tackle the whole wide world, though she be racked
                                                        with pain.

Could love be a feeling of a man for his wife, or a wife for her man,
Carrying them over the obstacles of life, like a gentle guiding hand,
Those feelings you have for dear Mum and Dad, who always
                                        guided your way,
With life's sacrifices gladly made for you, that helped make a better
day.

Could love be a feeling for your feathered or furry, ever friendly pet,
As they welcome you home excitedly, a better greeting you'll never get,
A greater loyalty and trust than this, for us humans is hard to find,
Sometimes surpassing that of your fellow man, could this be
                                                love of a kind?

Could love be those sharing times with your people, pride
                                        in your nation too,
Reflecting upon new landscapes, as they carry home her beauty to you,
Our feelings for one another, black, white, brown, yellow,
                                        maybe all stem from above
Finally burying our weapons of destruction forever, could this
                                        be the meaning of love?

Stuart Murray

THE SUN

I am the sun
I can chase away the rain
dry up the puddles
ease away your pain
I am the sun
I can burn your ropes
give back your dreams
recapture your hopes
I am the sun
and ever your friend
I will care for your heart
in time it will mend.

Catherine Sharpe

MY LOVE

Your smile, your laugh, your sense of fun
Are still a part of me
The cards you sent to make me smile
Are locked away safely

But what went wrong along the way
To spoil such happiness?
You went away, you hid your thoughts
Your private world, I guess

You're happy now, of that I'm sure
In this new life you have
But spare a thought just now and then
And think of me my love

We shared so much over the years
Don't throw all that away
Remember me and smile again
We'll meet again some day

Jill Myers

FOR JESSICA

I've witnessed your beauty
if only for a short while
and like falling in Paradise
I've tumbled into your smile.

I've seen the dawning of a new sun
and I've seen the smile on your face
I know which is the most beautiful one
I know which is the warmer place.

Your voice, an angel's choice
your innocent sparkling eyes
I question as to whether
they're really diamonds in disguise.

But I don't really know you
and you definitely don't know me
my shyness forces me to stay quiet
my longest speech is poetry.

So I ask you to stay Gold
'cause that's what you are
the day's yellowest sun
the night's brightest star.

Tomorrow you'll be gone
a new place for you to smile
and me, I'll just carry on
heartbroken, for a while.

Mark Norris

LOST AND ALONE

Everything seemed still that day,
Even the gulls that rose and fell
Above the girl seemed strangely quiet,
As if they knew these seconds were precious,
A sea mist settled on her face joining
The solitary tear which looked almost frozen there.
The memories of happier days seemed
Everywhere, and staring down at the foaming sea.
A light filled the eyes that would
Soon see no more, she smiled,
Then all was still.

Paul Gray

NO TITLE REQUIRED

Meet
Talk
Sex Sex Sex
Lies & Deceit
Shout
Argue
Fight
No More
The End

Michael Whittingham

LOVE TURNS

Love turns the sun into passions of fire
Turns admiration to desire
Rain is wine to dazzle and daze
A thick fog now a lover's haze
Dandelions are a bed of light
The smallest thing is one of height
Fruitful trees and buds go to flower
A unicorn becomes a stallion of power
Limp souls return from the dead
Drops of blood are an ocean of red
A vulture turns to a gentle dove
Roses represent the symbol of love
But they turn love into a mockery
They fade, wither and die.

Kath Wood

WHEN A MAN LOVES A WOMAN

As I think about you darling,
Can you not hear my plea?
Brighten up my darkest hour,
Please make a call to me.
To say that I am missing you,
Is simply not enough.
I never thought I'd feel this way
- Not of the sternest stuff!
Confession time is easy,
'I love you very much,'
Why else my heart beat rapidly
At your soft and gentle touch?
I asked the Lord to help me,
Where else was I to turn?
You only had to smile at me,
To make my passion burn.
I've made my feelings openly,
In fact I've bared my soul
This story of two players,
You have the leading role.
To love someone so deeply,
To get a second chance
Whatever fate may have in store,
I'll remember our last dance!

Terence G Bloodworth

To Love Forever

When will you sleep this heart of mine
That cries for love long lost?
When will you calm this heart of mine
And start to count the cost?

When will you see him as he is
And not as you would wish?
When will the conflict ever cease
And time erase his kiss?

When will my breast forget to ache
And fill with joy instead?
When will my eye be clear and still
And look for happiness ahead?

When will my heart not miss a beat
At mention of his name?
When will the memories stop their flow
And thoughts be gay again?

Not yet awhile I fear and dread.
The days are long and cold,
No solace yet for those who love
E'en tho' they may be old.

Will death bring joy and comfort then
When breast is still and done?
For then my love must quietly lie
And wait for him to come.

Eunice Doyle

ROGER . . . AND OUT

Just a short note to say,
That I missed you, today,
When I came round and knocked on your door,
I know that you said,
Last night, when I left,
That you wanted to see me no more.

But I still can't believe,
When you told me to leave
That the words that you spoke then, were true,
I just thought I'd make sure
And ask you once more,
If you really did mean we are through.

Your curtains moved,
Now, was that your cat,
Or are you inside, playing dead?
If you're not there, behind,
And you do change your mind,
You'll find me . . . drunk . . . in the 'Queen's Head.'

David Kellard

LOVE ISN'T

Within the mist of night your image comes to me.
I see your mask in black and white.
Living through my longest hour I want you.
From bud to flower, never opened before the mist
Of you.
Time has not altered my state of love.
Now I know what love is and there is nothing I
Can do.
Life fades by I feel I could die.

The mist brings your mask to me in black and white,
You set my world alight.
Alarm clock ticks and the feelings return.
I know my soul revolves around you.
There's no escape and there is nothing I can do,
The new flower still open waits for you.
What can I do?
Now I know what love is.

Lorraine Johns

TO BERNARD

We met in nineteen fifty one
I wonder where the years have gone?
You a cyclist tall and dark
I watched you race on Melbourne Park
Halesowen and Herne Hill too
Winning many events, I was proud of you
As members of Notts Castle Bicycle Club
We joined the Sunday run
Up and down the Derbyshire hills
We called it just good fun
Engaged in August nineteen fifty two
Came 20th December, I married you
Photographs taken in the pouring rain
Honeymoon in London, travelled by train
National Service beckoned
You went far away
To serve in the Royal Artillery
Not a happy day
Two years later your duty complete
Handed in your uniform
Back in civvy street
Two sons were born, Steve and Glenn
Soon became young boys, now young men
Forty-four years have passed
Our Wedding Anniversary is here
My love for you as ever
Deep and sincere.

Brenda M Hadley

POETRY IN MOTION

It's true that life
has its caresses
and life has its stings
and what you lose
on the roundabouts
you gain on the swings
but Anne when I'm with you
I gain on the swings
and the roundabouts too
and the slide
and the climbing frame
and the parallel bars
we punch away dark clouds
and reach up for stars
and if life is a playground
I want to keep playing with you
and jumping for joy
the woman the girl
the man the boy
because Anne when I'm with you
I gain on the swings
and the roundabouts too

Geoff Carder

NEVER FORGET

His footsteps sank deep in the rain soaked earth
Stones dug sharp into weary feet
The searing wind tore through his clothes
As onwards he plunged by sheer willpower

It was the strength of his mind that held him
Fast to that violent war-torn zone
Where to linger or dream was a dangerous game
Which could lead to the grave long before his time

An end of ideas, all hopes and ambitions,
Which seemed so bright just a year ago
A newly-wed with so much to strive for
But here and now just pain and fear.

Oh how could he tell her what it was like?
His letters told only what was wise to tell
She would worry still more, never sleep at night
If she knew what he knew on these foreign shores

He plunged on and on upwards and down
He stumbled and fell and rose again
Could that be his friend alone on the hill?
A youth of 18, now a man struck down.

Marjory Halton

LOVE

I am ever with you, even unto the end

Have no fear,
God is love
And is ever near.

A child can see
God is love,
So like a child I'll be.

In the beauty of nature
Love that is God
Banishes all care.

In my hour of need
Love that is God
Into comfort will me lead.

In every moment of care
The love of God
I know is there.

Florence Andrews

PASSION

A rustle of cloth in midnight hour
Rush of blood sweat on brow
Roaming hand mind of its own
Hot breath on face passionate moan
Fumbling fingers zipper down
Two bodies in ecstasy drown
Enveloped by dark of night
Combatants locking in frenzied fight
Sharpened talons' moonlit glow
Never knowing if friend or foe
To satisfy and animal need
A lust with which to sow a seed

D C Watkins

IS IT LOVE?

What is love, how can we say
Is it a feeling that won't go away.
The heart that races when you meet,
So fast you'll think it stops its beat
The look you get when your eyes set
Upon one whose love you can't forget.
Every emotion is at high and on cue
And jealousy plays its part too.

The endless thoughts when you are apart
Wishing one near with all your heart
To hold in your arms once again
And try to make it out, but in vain,
No-one can resist when caught in it
You are carried along as though adrift
So why is it love, how can this be,
Why and how it makes a fool of me.

E P Devereux

TRUST

You'd better not be taking me for a ride.
What I feel for you, do you feel inside?
You say you care,
You're always there.
But how do I know,
You're not on the go
Behind my back?
Do I cut too much slack?
Don't ever leave me,
That would sure grieve me.
You'd better not be taking me for a ride.
Am I caught once more on love's downward slide?
Are you fooling me?
Does this love hold three?
And while I'm away
Do you still swear you'll stay
When the other dogs come sniffing round your tree?
Will you still hold back and wait for me?

Robert Crisp

FIRST LOVE

Today is your birthday -
You were my first love.

Are you still alive, I wonder.
Retired maybe, like me?

You filled my youth
With tingle-touch excitement.

I wrote poems for you -
But you broke my heart.

Beatrice Ewart

RICHES

Love is pairing and sharing, wearing child-bearing,
Smiling and grinning while losing or winning,
Love is flurry and scurry, or calming great worry
Of money, not funny, but grafting brings honey.
Love is caring or swearing, flaring rage blaring,
Rowing and hissing, to bear-hugging, kissing.
Love is fun and exciting, kids biting, in-fighting,
Then war starts to thaw lulled to order of law.
Love is teenagers stinking of bravado drinking,
They do not tarry, move out, maybe marry.
Love is a quietness unknown, when at last we're alone.
Rich freedom about, eat in or dine out?
But:
Love's silence is broken by grandchild awoken,
The kids have not flown, they keep bouncing back home.
Love is ageless and priceless, life toothless and fruitless
Without life's best date with the world's greatest mate.

Hilary Robson

LOVE COULD . . . LIFE COULD

Love could make poets of us all,
if only we would let it.
But if we did, what would befall
all those who are indebted,
for inspiration to love's call,
so they can write, to please us all,
of passions pure and otherwise,
soft words, flowers, clear blue skies?

Would they then resort to writing about sensible things
in order to keep their bank balances in the black?

And life could make cynics of us all!
'I love you!' Have you heard it?
And will it be painful to recall,
in some future, how absurd it
is that once, though you both knew it
to be love, you would not hold it,
but with oily words and anger,
as if possessed, you threw it
all away?

Brian Cox

THE DAY I LAST SAW YOU

They turned the lights out in the world
The day I last saw you,
And all the sea went darkest grey instead of azure blue.
A shroud of purple velvet is covering my heart.
Oh why did you decide to leave? I thought we'd never part.
A silver moonbeam showed us the stairway to the stars
We sped across the universe and stopped to gaze at Mars.
Our joys when we were together could fill an ocean wide
So why dispel the happiness and start the ache inside?
I pray your newest love affair will fade like autumn leaves
And if it does remember me, the one whose love reveals
A fervent heart that's warm and true, a heart that thinks
The world of you!

Philomena Dunlop

WHISPERING DREAMS

It's okay
Time will pass
(Reliable as always)
And everything I felt -
Everything you stirred -
Will just fade away.

Was it only this time yesterday
That I closed my eyes with you?
Crazy dreams for crazy times,
Crazy schemes and crazy crimes.
In our embrace what did we say?
The oldest words all rang true.
But then, they always do.

It's okay
Time will hold our promises
For another occasion,
Perhaps when there is a better equation
To whisper our mad mad dreams -
The dreams that all lovers hold.

Peter James Warr

ETERNALLY

Shall I take you to my bed
Leave all the special things unsaid?
Will you warm and comfort me,
Hold me tight, or let me be?
Scents of skin and hair so fresh,
Eyes so tender, then caress.
You might not want a tender touch,
But being there just means so much.
When you look into my eyes,
Whisper softly, or tell me lies,
As long as you belong to me,
My life, my love, eternally.

E J Metcalfe

WHAT DOES BECOME OF THE BROKEN-HEARTED?

How could I have been so naive,
To believe that love could bring happiness and joy?
I found someone,
Several people, who I believed truly loved me for who I am.
I trusted in them, believed in them,
Only to find out they never really cared.

What really hurts is that they pretended they cared,
And what's more I believed them.

Love should bring smiles and laughter,
For me only tears and heartache.

I look at love with scorn,
For all my beliefs had been placed in that one word,
Only for my world to be crushed by those who I had loved.

How can people be so cruel?
To say they care one minute,
Then disregard me the next as if I'm nothing,
Nothing more than a piece of litter,
Which they can pick up and drop as they please.

I thought friendship was something never-ending,
Lasting through good and bad,
When their love was tested,
I was left all by myself.

One by one I've seen my friendships slip away,
And although I remain with outstretched arms,
No-one wants me or my love.

Love is always painted with roses,
But what about those,
Who have lost all faith,
Fearing the consequences of being able to love again?

Ms Beckett

ROMANTIC VALENTINE

You are my chosen Valentine,
Because you are sweeter than wine,
Love that is complete, is so sweet,
I will be yours, you will be mine.

The moment you came my way,
You made that day my lucky day,
Life together, will last forever,
Our hearts will never go astray.

I want our love to last forever,
Not just a passing moment of pleasure,
You are a queen, the girl of my dreams,
You are my most precious treasure.

You are the one I have chose,
To you and only you will I propose,
When you are with me, it feels like ecstasy,
That is why I give you a Valentine rose.

I know it now as I knew from the start,
That from your love I will never part,
The power of love, is from heaven above,
You will always have a place in my heart.

Robin R Robinson

DESIRE WITHIN

She's there, but she's not.
We sit not yards apart,
Yet the gulf between us is immeasurable,
From time to time our gaze meets,
Yet each hastily looks away,
No connection, yet feelings well up,
Love, anger, resentment, frustration and joy,
All interwoven in the mind of man.

One part of me longs to sever,
This hope of one day holding her,
Yet still another side clings,
With the clutches of a dying man,
To the desire within.
Oh to forget, the joy not yet known,
But the heart knows no reason,
There is no logic in love.

Is she aware of my inner struggle?
Does she care or ever think of me?
Hope maintains she does,
But hope can fade,
Yet I don't want it to
Better to hold on to possibility,
Than live in a world full of doubt,
Maybe sometimes reality and dreams concur.

James Erskine

LOVE

In the outer reaches of your mind
You will hear a distant drum,
Pulsating crazily through your heart,
In uneven equilibrium.

Re-directing every plan you've made,
Your adrenaline will run high;
You will think your world's your oyster
As you reach out to the sky.

There will be no rationality
In anything you do,
Lost hope and fear, that once was near,
Have vanished in the blue.

You will walk along delightful paths,
Throw caution to the wind.
And see your life for what it is,
With unfettered peace of mind.

So what is this transition,
This magic from above;
It's the elementary gift from God,
It's pure, it's great! It's love.

Gerry Concah

FORBIDDEN FRUIT

I saw you today.
You looked very briefly my way.
My heart it raced at such a speed.
Our bodies ached with unfilled need,
It's lust I know and oh so wrong,
My heart to another does belong.
I want you oh God how I need you,
Please tell me you want me too.
A wedding ring upon my finger,
I know - I know it's wrong to linger.
You are already spoken for.
Is that what makes us want each other more?
Erotic thoughts run freely through my mind,
Wracked with guilt am I being so unkind?
Can I help if my love for another has died,
You have no idea how much I've cried.
Together we have tasted the forbidden fruit,
Both of us knowing this is the wrong route.
A new passion has awoken inside of me.
Oh how I wish we could set it free.
We have snatched this hour to be together,
So hold me my darling it can't be forever.

Suzanne Monk-Arnold

VALENTINE

People have been looking at me strangely
because I'm walking on air

Passers-by stop and sing the snowman song
but really I don't care

Cloud nine is where you will find me
should I float away

Tomorrow I look forward to
the love I found today

Janet Slater

THE DEATH OF LOVE

The bride was so radiant on her special day
Little did she know of the tears which ahead of her lay
Her life until then had been one of love and laughter
How could she know it would not last ever after?

Her heart was full of love and the wish to be a good wife
To the one she loved she would dedicate her life
All she knew was how to love, be truthful and kind
She was not prepared by life for the demons in his mind

What was it in him that meant she had to be denigrated
Deep inside him festered some deep dark hatred
She had so willingly placed herself in his power
When between them a wonderful love had seemed to flower

When joyously embarking on her new life she did not know
                                          there would come the day
When with a motley crowd in some downbeat bar he would rather stay
Staggering home, with tongue or hand he would her lash
All her hopes of a happy, loving life he would dash

Through all his rages and the constant verbal abuse
She sought and sought to make for him every feeble excuse
Life for a man in the outside world could be so hard
She had to show him that at home he was held in high regard

She was always faithful, loving, and turning the other cheek
All she did was to put herself at his mercy, helpless and weak
After enduring his unjustified raging, year after year
She became too deeply unhappy to shed even a tear

Then one day when the terrible abuse from his mouth did spew
With a sudden clarity of thought she at last knew
With feelings she had never allowed in her head so fully
She had wasted all these years with a foul-mouthed bully

The battered, bruised body of love gave a whimper and died

Margaret Meagher

THE OLD DESIRE

When I was young and love-replete
The fruits of life were ever sweet;
When I am old, that tired refrain
Shall fade, till only dreams remain.

But visions yet materialise
To light the past in present eyes,
And fact and fantasy conspire
To rouse me to the old desire.

The old desire is with me still,
Unquenched of flame and strong of will;
And so, with siren-throated sigh,
Love sings, 'ere joy and beauty die.

Stephen H Smith

LOVE

Love passed by unsuspected
like an unfamiliar song
never knew what was expected,
didn't know the dice were thrown.
That they were fully laden
as they rolled across the board,
love's often been mistaken
as a friendship; nothing more.

It could be a wild adventure
like the first steps on the moon,
when you catch the kiss that love has signed
as it floats across the room.
To let your heart start beating
as if a child that's newly born.
Given time love turns a cygnet
into a full grown swan.

It's part of life; forever
is a treasure to be saved.
Not measured like the sands of time.
Love lives beyond the grave.
You share it whilst in Heaven
it's given as a gift,
for you, for me, for everyone
that you want to share it with.

Alan Glendinning

THE LOVE WE SHARED

I don't know if I can walk away from you,
Walk away from the love we shared
It seems so long ago
We used to walk, and talk, and love
Oh-how we loved - do you remember
The love we shared?

It's sad that love can die
But worse to watch its death throes
Better to leave now, while we are still friends,
Before all the good disappears from
The love we shared

Is she so much better than me?
What can she give?
Love, care, unconditionally. I have tried
Perhaps that is the problem with
The love we shared

When did we erect this barrier, this wall
Which threatens to fall and crush us?
Now run - don't look back
Upon
The love we shared

Rose Rendell

BUTTERFLY

Wing your way now
To my dear Kate
And let her know
There's not long left
For her to wait
I'll see her soon

And tell her this
We'll walk among the trees
And lie
In open fields

And place this kiss
Upon her lips
So she may know
How much I've missed
These winter days
Her sweet embrace
Her gentle touch
Her trusting face

She is my day
She is my night
She is my way
And its guiding light

So fare thee well
Go tell my Kate

Sharam Gill

SORROW

In the last darkness, entwined her lips and mine
There all was shadow and breaths were past
And upon my soul the kisses were lost in time;
But I was desiring the touch of a passion old,
Yes, I was desiring the one who was last:
I have been unfaithful and so I just feel cold.

All night my body could feel another's heartbeat,
And while dark advanced in my arms she lay;
And to all but me her kisses would feel so sweet;
But I was desiring the touch of a passion old,
And when I awoke I found the sky was grey:
I have been unfaithful and so I feel just cold.

In a short time I have lost much from my mind,
Past moments and joys do throng,
Absent now, blown like a feather on the wind,
For I was desiring the touch of a passion old,
And yes I cry through the dance as not long:
For I have been unfaithful and so I feel just cold.

I pray for more days of love and stronger wine,
But when the candle burns down the love expires,
And so falls the shadow of end when the night is thine;
For still I desire the touch of a passion old,
And yes I crave the lips of lost desire:
For I have been unfaithful and so I feel just cold.

Shaun Jeffery

TO LOVE SOMEONE

Love can be a blessing,
It can also be a pain,
Love can keep you guessing
You either lose or gain

But love is also beautiful,
If shared by both of you,
When you are together
And you know that love is true

When you love somebody,
And you're true with all your heart,
Nothing in this world can ever
Pull your love apart.

Always tell your loved one,
You love them every day,
Never let the sun go down
On anger - that's not the way.

Keep the interest going,
By looking neat and smart,
Then never can you give away
Your true and loving heart

Love *will* be a blessing,
If will *never* be a pain,
If you try to love each other
Come sunshine, snow or rain.

Joyce Hammond

LOVE

Love - a quiet understanding
Ebbing and flowing with the tide,
Leaving ripples on the water,
Like the sands of time.

Love - so many different feelings,
Passion or the gentle touch of a hand,
A smile or lilting laughter
Brings a peace of mind.

Love - cruel as the sea
Or kind as a dove in full flight,
All these feelings nurtured, treasured,
Mark the glow of life.

Doreen McDonald Banks

OLD BIG BEN

God bless old Big Ben
The unchanging friend,
Standing majestically in Westminster Palace
Amid pomp and circumstance,
World politics and upheavals.

With amazing grace
She keeps timing and chiming along;
In all changing scenes of life
Through all kinds of weather
Rock firm she stands as ever.

Worth her weight in gold and prestige
How we would miss her if she fell ill
The loveliest clock ever
To grace the City of Westminster.
A national institution she is
Renowned the world over for her dignity,
Striking and chiming ability.
God bless old Big Ben!
She's a wonderful gem.

Katie Kent

True Love

Oceans of love like the tide of time,
Heavenly kisses that make you mine.
Each tender caress as our soft lips meet,
As our bodies entwine with emotional heat.

Love's sweet aroma all around in the air,
Mixed with the perfumed smell of your hair.
The radiant rush of your warm glowing cheek,
As our pleasure soars to the highest peak.

I promise, my dear, I will always be true,
As my body and soul now belong to you,
Caring and sharing until death us do part,
I offer my love and give you my heart.

Sandra Balfour

LOVE AND MARRIAGE

You will be married,
Before me,
We laid together,
My girlfriend and I,
Then my future husband
Came along.

What's the bet,
Will he like me,
Or will he like you?
I won, we fell,
In love,
And we were one.

We must get married,
You are too young,
I love him,
He will love and protect me,
Nothing will change me,
I love him.

Barbara Brown

What Shall I Do?

What shall I do about you?
If I asked a friend,
They'd say it's not true,
That no-one could feel the way
        that I do,
O, what shall I do about you?

What should I do with your smile?
When thinking about it
Time and awhile
It sets my heart racing mile after mile,
O, what should I do with your smile?

What should I do with your kiss?
For there's nothing at all
That I would more miss
Of memories of you the first
        would be this,
O, what shall I do with your kiss?

And what shall I do with your love?
If I was without it
Heavens above!
I am the hand and you are the glove,
O, What shall I do with your love?

Vince Evans

LOVE

What is love?
Love is a feeling as high as the ceiling
or a dynamic force that leaves your sense reeling

Love is wanting to say yes but having to say no
or whispering yes and then letting you go

Love is a hug from someone you love very much
or sometimes it can simply be a stranger's touch

Love is a pleasant smile during a harassing day
or maybe a caring word you hear somebody say
Because
Love is never cruel, it doesn't stare or compare
it's full of goodness, it wants to care and to share

Love doesn't hate, it ignores those who intimidate
and love never gets angry, irritable or irate

Love is never spiteful, it doesn't call people names
no matter what the wrong, love never blames

Love doesn't stamp and shout, asking you to explain
it sheds quiet tears, forgiving again and again

Michael D Kearney

CRYING FOR YOU

Every lonely captured rainbow,
Carries away a part of me.
Flowing from a selfish soul,
As love could never match a dream.

Jill Scorer

THANK YOU

We met, we loved, we married, he was
The ideal man for me, he cherished and
Protected me, from life's unhappy knocks, he
Made me laugh, and sometimes cry, he made
Me happy, he made me sigh, he never forgot
Those special dates, there was always a
Surprise beside my plate, he was not
Exactly handsome, but to me he was everything
The moon, the stars, rolled into one, now I'm
Bereft because he's gone, I wish that I'd said
'Thank you' for the love he gave to me, he
Showed it in so many ways, he never expected
Or received any praise - now I want to say
'Thank you' a little late maybe, for the gift
Of love you gave me, and the love I have for thee.

Katherine Ney

LOVE

The twinkle in your eyes
the smile on your face
being with you
makes it a wonderful place.
You're someone very special
your love you share
the comfort you bring
I'm glad you care.
My life without you
could never be the same
you brought me happiness
how glad I am you came.
I hope you never leave
if that time came
my heart you would thieve
my happiness you'd take too.

Charlene Whelan

LOVE IS

Love is feeling as if my blood
is sparkling crystal water.
It is jumping for joy
and soaring up to touch
the inverted blue bowl
of the sky.
It is sprouting soft wings,
soaring over fields and rivers;
reaching horizons, kissing rainbows.
Love is flying high. Love is you.

Sue Johnson

THOUGHTS OF YOU

I, am not dead,
I live,
I have constant thoughts
Of you,
You, are here,
Beside me,
In everything I do.

You, are not dead.
This I know,
For I hear of you,
From everyone I know.

They, take pleasure,
In telling me,
Of the way you are,
But, I will never
Stop loving you,
For I really care.

So some time,
On a winter's night,
When you are snug
And warm,
Think of me,
For many times, I
Think of you,
Until the break of dawn.

Brian Morris

HEART AND MIND

Now and then
I look to see,
So glad am I to find,
The very special
Love so sweet,
That joins us,
            Heart and mind.

M J P Durbidge

VALENTINE BOUQUET OF FLOWERS

Love is like a valentine bouquet of flowers,
Love is when it is fresh,
Love is when it blossoms and grows.
Love is when it grows old,
Love hurts when it withers and dies,
Love hurts when your loved one dies.
Love hurts when you are left,
And all you can do is cry.
Love hurts when your teardrops fall,
Like when the petals of the flowers fall and die.

Margaret Coleman

TORN BETWEEN TWO

Torn between two
Which one really loves you
The one that's with you day and night
Or the one that you turn to
When you've had a fight?

Comparing them all the time
Why can't you get them
Out of your mind?

Can't let go of either you see
I feel that they belong to me
To see either with another girl
Would hurt too much
And cause my heart to bust.

I love them both in different ways
But I need to make my mind up
Before they stray
From my heart
As there's not room for two
But it's just so hard
To say goodbye
To either of you.

Natasha Mealing

ALONE

The darkness grips me,
My stomach churns,
Emptiness envelops me
In its all-encompassing coldness.
What have I done to earn such treatment,
To be abandoned, alone and tired?

Each day passes dully
Though the sun may shine.
Each night is silent,
Quiet, apart from my weeping.
Tears bring no comfort from the overwhelming lonesomeness
As I curl up protecting myself from the world.

Thoughts crowd my mind,
Questions, all unanswered.
Does he want me to write,
To phone or to speak?
Should I try to visit and risk rejection?
Be hurt through and through and never find peace?

Keep away in the distance,
Cable not on the wire,
Make silence the order
To not cause discord.
He knows where I am, caring as ever,
Awaiting his message to tell me he lives.

Patricia Farrer

I KNOW, I'M SURE, IT MUST BE LOVE

Because I still ask questions, I know it must be love
Because I have no answers, I'm sure it must be love
I look at you and wonder and I know it must be love
When you are in my presence, I'm sure it must be love
For when you're here, we feel as one and I know it must be love
And when you're gone, I'm one, but not, and I'm sure it must be love
The years we've had, they've raced on by, and so it must be love
The bad we've had has never lasted and so it must be love
I cannot understand it, but I guess it must be love
I cannot touch nor hold it, but I'm sure it must be love
For somehow I can feel it and I know it must be love
But what is love, how can I know, if that I do not know
Because I still ask questions, I'm sure it must be love.

Linda Romain

LOVE

Love is a silly thing
That makes you happy
And sad.
Makes you laugh makes you
Cry.
I wonder why?

The first kiss is a bliss
The first date you cannot wait
Is your hair in place or your
Figure the right shape?
Does your make-up look right?
I wonder why?

Holding hands making love
Being together through all the days
Planning a holiday away.
Oh what is it like to be in love?
Going to the pictures or down the pub,
It doesn't matter as you have your man.

Linda Bevan

RECIPE FOR LOVE

The security of a happy home,
From which I never wish to roam,
The laughter of happy children at play,
Excitedly talking, growing each day
The miracle of a babe newly born,
The sun slowly rising on a bright clear morn,
Brightly coloured flowers swaying in the breeze
Birds, animals, insects, rain and the trees,
Love, contentment, happiness, health
All outnumber worldly wealth.
Into the basin pour one and a half pounds of love
Stir in gently the things you're dreaming of.
Add half a pound of laughter and a pinch of real good fun.
Throw in some children add them one by one.
A spoon of contentment an ounce of give and take
Do not boil, or a mishap you will make.
Add one hundred kisses, maybe a little fewer,
Stir very gently, leave a few years to mature.
If you follow this recipe through happiness and strife
You will live a long, happy and enjoyable life.

Win Cook

I WANT

I want to watch you smile
as I enter the room.
I want to join in with your life,
and be close to you.
I want to meet your friends,
let them see me.
I want to be in love,
but I wants, don't get.

Alex Wardle

THE WIFE

I always thought our love would last
But now I know it's in the past.
Sometimes I sit, and wonder why
My love for you would ever die.
I would really like to go away,
But in my heart I know I'll stay.
So I'll just get on with my life
And be a loyal, caring wife.

Janet Stephens

VALENTINE

Today,
I will give you
a 1000 kisses,
each one spiced with ginger,
then delicately wrapped
in rice paper.
One by one,
I will place them
on your tongue,
then watch you
close your eyes,
as you feel them melt,
their heat
burning your lips
searing your mind.

H R Burns

IT'S OVER

'It's over.' He had told her
In a busy rush hour queue.
She wanted to talk it over
In his cold rented rooms.

The door had opened and shut
Before he even remembered
She was going to call.
Silence stood between them.

Her eyes were darkly shining
Her hair was long and straight
Her boots were old and muddy
Her dress was shroudlike pale.

The back way was discreet
No-one would have seen her.
He had finished with her.
So now she finished with him.

'It's over.' He had told her
And she'd thought him heartless
Still the blood was plenty,
She threw away her dress.

Alison Crawford-Ward

PARTING IN PAIN

I try so hard to understand that all this wasn't really planned.
Although splitting up's become a trend I love you more than any friend.
'Please bear with me' is what you say, and I wait for your
phone call, every day.
But you could never really know, how much this hurts and pains me so.
If only you had understood, I meant this love to last for good.
And now you've gone and left me here, every day, I shed a tear.
With every tear that stains my face, there's another one, to take its
place,
This love, I feel is all for you, but you have torn this heart in two.
I lay alone at night in bed with thoughts of you, inside my head.
I pray to God each night and day, that he might bring you back my way.
I sometimes wish my heart would die. Then I would have no need
to sit and cry.
As I sit here feeling low, there's something, I want you to know.
With every single passing day, no-one else could make me feel this
way.
My love runs deep, so deep inside. My feelings, I find hard to hide.
Though you're with her instead of me, I'll love you till eternity.
I'm sorry, if this makes you sad, but sometimes I feel so very bad.
I wish that I could turn back time, back to when you were all mine.

Susan Adams

PROPOSAL?

'Ask me to marry you,'
I once said - joking;
but when you caught me off guard
I knew you meant it -
'I want it to work -
please, be my wife;
I want you, I need you
I love you,' you said.
What changed these words
from happiness to sorrow?
What changed your feelings -
and the way you touched me?
'Be mates!' you said,
'we know it won't work.
At least we know
that we love
each other!'
That broke my heart.

Kirsty Phillips

FORBIDDEN LOVE

A forbidden love began burning bright
Emotions ran high, it felt so right
But what felt right was deemed so wrong
Because to someone else she did belong
Snatched moments came and passions ran high
The tears did fall when they said goodbye
The goodbyes became too hard to bear
They knew that they should end the affair
But their feelings just grew even stronger
Their love they felt they could hide no longer
Two families' lives did become entwined
New sons and daughters each did find
Their lives would never again be the same
Their love burning bright, was in fact a flame
A flame that several had tried to blow out
But in their minds there was no doubt
Together forever is where they would be
Caring and sharing until eternity

Helen Bealing

KATE IN 1950

How I wish I'd known you in nineteen-fifty!
Red your hair, your face of a milky softness,
Bright your eyes and naughty your smile as always,
      Bored by The Season,
Talking only about your horse, and I'd have
Longed to ride beside you and love your freckles.
I'd have talked of Keats and of course of Homer,
      And you'd have listened,
- And the Beeb of course, and of carriage-cleaning.
Then we'd have leapt up to the teeming dance-floor,
And the Danube then would have flowed in Yorkshire
      Or else in Caithness.

Angus Sinclair

BLAME

Forward was never so backward nor awkward to be,
Flying in dazes so alien to me,
So was it the sun or the stars or the sky
Which turned round your promise to a solemn goodbye?

Perhaps 'twas the trees or the grass or the blooms
Which sentenced our lives to solitary gloom,
Or maybe the clouds or the rain or the snow
Which put out the candle in an icyswift blow.

Could it be me or could it be you?
Perhaps it was something we're going to do,
Or maybe the thing that we cannot rein tight,
The ultimate force we're unable to fight,

Or maybe the fact we're forbidden to be
Together, forever and eternity.
What was the cause I really can't say,
Life has a habit of working that way.

G T Crump

LOVE

Love comes to everyone in some shape or form
Whether a new born baby or a lover on your arm
Senses and feelings can passionately heighten
Eyes and hearts that seem to brighten
Fond words, a touch, a little smile
Glances and scents, a young child's guile.
Cosiness, softness and warm sunshine's rays
Tastes and smells that linger for days
Palpitations and hearts that flutter
Joyous feelings at baby's first mutter
Sensations, desires tenderest emotions
Rose petals, flowers and herbaceous lotions
People who say love's like a sweet dream
Faraway countries and places we've been
Next time you see someone with a fond smile
Think of your loved ones and ponder a while.
Sharing fond memories of the emotions above,
They're all different meanings of everyone's love.

Estelle Anderson

TRUE LOVE

You can never describe the feelings of true love,
The pain you feel is so hurtful,
How does anything compare to heartache,
And how can anyone repair a broken heart.

Your first love is always the best,
New feelings, new energy, new enthusiasm,
But when it's gone there's nothing,
Except an empty space in your heart.

'Love hurts' is what they say,
I can relate to that,
When love's gone there's emptiness,
As the arrow pierces a hole in your heart.

All of a sudden it seems the whole world's against you,
But you just want to be left alone,
Emotions and thoughts which were forever,
Are now a figure of your imagination.

Emma Snell (16)

UNTIL WE BOTH . . .

I shall wait
For my soul-mate,
Though many a year go by:

For somewhere in heaven
There is a leaven
To each man's and maid's sigh:

And the day will come
When delirium
Will descend unto them anigh:

Therefore my soul-mate
Will me, too, await,
Until we, both, one another stupefy . . . !

R John Austin

THE POWER OF LOVE

It's love that makes the world go round
So the old saying goes
Without it life would be so drab
Monotonous . . . full of woes.
Love comes in many different forms
To fill our lives with joy
The love a mother gives her child
The love twixt girl and boy.
The love that stands the test of time
That saves us from despair
When all around seems dark and grim
We find that love is there.
Love is the greatest gift of all
So grasp it while you may
Then share this love with those you meet
As you traverse life's way.

Gwyneth D Futer

LOOKING INTO OPHELIA'S WINDOW

And now to you, my fair Ophelia,
locked in a world of icy cold
Did you ever meet your true love
or chance to find a heart of gold?

As you lie alone until the sunset
with just your thoughts for company
Do you ever yearn for passions
that for you could never be?

Out to work at nine each morning
and home alone at half past three
Perhaps an hour in church on Sunday
could never be enough for me

I never reached your high ideals
nor lived up to your purity
And we never climbed upon that mountain
to find what you would never see

Those soft clothes on your body
might just as well be steel
Spun tight by bitter memories
on some Arctic spinning wheel

But I carry with me still a vision,
of things that might have come to be
Had those dark eyes of flashing beauty
ever seen a future free

A J Marchant

IT'S A JOY WHEN WE KISS!

It's a joy when we kiss.
It's a moment,
When we tingle and fizz.
We can tell the world,
We know what love is.
It's a joy when we kiss!

It's a joy when we smile.
We are happy,
Every inch, every mile.
We'd be together,
If we could all the while.
It's a joy when we smile!

Well you know,
I'm always thinking of you,
And forever this will be.
All my words of love,
You know they are true.
I have written them down,
For everyone to see.

It's a joy when we share.
Our loving friendship,
Shows that we care.
We know together,
We can feel love is there.
It's a joy when we share!

My love for you, I know,
Will be forever.
You're the only girl for me.
I want to be with you,
And leave you never.
Every time I look,
I hope you're there to see.

It's a joy when we kiss.
A treasured moment,
When we tingle and fizz.
We can show the world,
We know what love is.
It's a joy when we kiss!
It's a joy when we kiss!
Such bliss it is!

Graham Mitchell

I GUESS THEY CALL IT LOVE

Two hands that touch when dining.
Slight misting of the eyes.
That glance that says 'You're special'
A warmth you can't disguise.
These symptoms, oh so painful
Whenever you're apart
Produce likewise, most strongly,
A tugging at the heart.
. . . I guess romance's pundits call it love.

Those feelings of elation
Just walking hand in hand.
That empathy of spirit, that
True partners understand.
Dire symptoms, oh so hurtful
When thoughtless words are said
Which churn up inner feelings
That perhaps romance is dead.
. . . I guess such fears are simply part of love.

A gift you weren't expecting.
That sudden sunny smile.
Shared secret lovers' nicknames
To comfort and beguile.
Such symptoms, oh so blissful
Will never fade away
When two hearts fuel a passion
That warms each passing day.
. . . I guess if all this happens, it means love.

Richard J Bradshaw

SYMPHONY FOR A BLUE BOY

My blue boy lies in Morpheus' arms now
I hide memories under the wardrobe
Wishing to crawl into half-light
As you and I once were.

My blue boy sleeps with angels now
Loved in a different room with the same haircut.
I used to wait in the wings for my life
Now I can be centre stage.

My blue boy resists spotlights now:
'But why did we lie together
in a tangle of life never understood?'
I cried upon my pillow.

My blue boy holds me to his heart, now
I feel warm and secure.
Having an understanding of what it means to love
Believing in the everlasting.

My blue boy passed away, still
part of us is together floating
in the ether, a street lamp serenade . . .
'The Symphony of a Blue Boy'.

Nick Brunel

INDEPENDENTLY UNAWARE

I thought I'd never fall in love
well, not again
I've been there, bought the T-shirt,
felt the pain
Sometimes I had the urge
went to night-clubs, stood on my own,
left on my own, went home and cried
Other times I'd stand with a crowd
shouting into blokes' ears, the music was always too loud
I soon tired of that
and took up other interests
like taking root in front of the TV
while eating ice cream
But after switching it off at bedtime
deafening loneliness made me want to scream.
I had to pull myself together,
survive on my own, at ease with my company
preferred being alone
Of course I have lots of friends
and they made amends
I even had the odd fleeting fling
but they didn't feel right
and never lead to anything.
Getting on with my life, independent and strong
What goes and happens? He comes along
crept up unexpectedly, was I ready for this?
Admiration, respect and this weirdly peaceful bliss?
Like I said, I never thought I'd fall in love . . .
not again.

Michelle Harris

UNTITLED

You carve your love (yourself) upon me,
Each year I look within and find it deeper,
Each moment smoothes a curve or cuts anew
For it is a sculpture with no final shape
For our love is to continue . . .

Louise Shapland

BEST FRIENDS

The man and the woman looked at the sea.
he said, 'I will always be there for thee,
but no . . . I will not write.
But you have to write to me, I depend upon it.'

She was hurt and dismayed.
This cannot be . . .
The written word is vital to me.
It is something I depend on!

She didn't write, did not write.

A complete year past, and then she wrote.
Her life was a mess, and she hoped, he would be
there for her.
As he had said he would be . . . the year before.

The phone rang . . .
'I am sorry about your job,' he said.
'Your being alone, made my soul shed a tear for thee.
And I am here as promised.'

Sheila Mack

Unleashed (A Prayer)

Passion, permit me an understanding,
A vicarious indulgence of love;
Allow this novice, this tempered victim,
A rare insight in the name of penance.
I've seen, heard and scented the victory,
Once it trailed teasingly on my tongue,
But never have I held, without constraint,
Without foolish doubt, love's embodiment.
I will not sell myself to your spirit,
Selling cheapens; I give myself to you.
I will not divide myself for favour,
Such experience must be savoured whole.
I will not, cannot, accept you in faith,
Faith is not an issue of your credence;
Substance however, is testimony,
A demonstration beyond temptation,
And yet, my patience I owe to belief
And patience is my only worthwhile strength.
I have always wanted more and given all,
And oft I've received more than I deserve.
Still, I want to touch the ultimate love,
A mutual unquestioned empathy.
Supplier of strength, witness to my faults,
Laugh with me, lay with me, put up with me.
I'm yours.

Byron Katt

STEPHEN

Stephen took me walking in a perfect field of corn.
The sun blazed down upon us: there had been no clouds since dawn.
His kisses spoke sincerity and love beyond compare,
And beneath the laughing summer skies I wandered without care.

As we'd sat one evening underneath the sky so wide,
The starlight lit his eyes, and he'd asked me to be his bride.
He'd offer me his life, he said, if I could pledge my own;
And in me, love was blooming now from seeds which he had sown.

I loved him - Lord, I loved him - as we moved into the shade,
But only with my soul: with bodies, love was never made.
I felt I'd given everything which true love could require -
We dwelt together peacefully with no force of desire.

He sat me down.
The traffic moved on scorched roads far away.
I waited eagerly for words of love I hoped he'd say.
He spoke of love, as I had guessed -
But not of love for me:
He told me that another gave herself more readily.

The traffic moved, but my world stopped -
Until I turned and fled.
I lost the path, but didn't care: love's rose too soon was dead.
He'd hurled away my greatest gift, and paid me back in lies;
And the sun blazed without mercy from the laughing summer skies.

Alex Louise West

SOMEONE FOR ME

I need to find myself a man
A man who will understand
When I'm happy and when I'm sad
When I'm upset and when I'm mad

A man who knows love's stronger than pride
And whose feelings for me he will not hide
And who will look after me and always take care
And be there for me, when life's not fair

I want him to be my lover and also be my friend
So I can rely on him when I need a hand to lend
I want him to love me for just being me
Because this is the way I'll always be

I want to be able to spend some quality time
With him holding me saying 'you're mine'
I want to be able to say 'I love you'
Because those occasions have been so very few

I want a strong man who will sweep me away
And special things to me will only say
Someone to share the lonely nights and hold me tight
Someone, who for me, who will put up a fight

I want someone by my side who will always stay
And to promise me he'll never go away
Someone who'll love me, no matter what
Because this is me, this is all I've got.

Tina Taylor

FOR YOUR LOVE

For your love I'd walk a thousand miles,
And for your love a thousand more.
For you I'd swim the furthest ocean,
Only stopping at the shore,
For your love I'd climb the highest mountain,
Thro' thunder, lightning, rain and snow,
And for your love I'd hold you close
And never want to let you go.
All these things I'd do for you
And many, many, many more.
To be with you until I die contented
And happy and so secure.

The key inside my heart is yours forever and a day
I'll never change the lock on you and never run away,
And when you're not around me
All I think about is you, you are my one and only love,
Miss Barnes you no it's true, so be with me forever
And make my life and world real sweet,
I'll love you for eternity babe,
          With you my life's complete.

Paul Cushen

LIKE RAIN

I thought of you on your birthday.
I thought of trying to explain,
But, faltering searching speeches
Would only make you uneasy,
So I went to play in the rain;
Walking the hand-held routes we walked,
Those I have walked countless since,
Slipping on the dog-shit of sense,
To cleanse in puddles of mem'ry
All love's acts that made me weary,
Made you wary with disbelief;
Sometimes attention is like rain:
　　　　You get soaked unperceiving,
　　　　Or drenched by sudden downpours.
　　　　From my gentle eyes and kiss
　　　　You expected light showers
　　　　But, instead, I was a storm.
If I could cup-up all my words
And let them trickle through my hands
To run like droplets and cascade,
As kisses did, passion warm skin,
Would you understand, any more,
Events preceding our brief time,
How my vuln'rability tried
To wash you free of doubt, like rain?

Martin K

THE HAND OF FATE

Who was it poised the hand of fate
That struck, with mighty force, to break
All steadfast resolutions?
The thoughts that made me vow to trust
No man again, in love or lust.
Who shattered those illusions?

But, who could tell, of those within
That room, my life would just begin
Through one, a stranger, entering?
Because the hands of fate did strike,
Two lives, together now unite;
Two hearts, as one are beating!

Sandra Wolfe

'TWAS LOVE THAT BROUGHT US TOGETHER

'Twas love that brought us together,
And love will keep us together,
Whatever be the weather;
We will always stay together.

Love bind us together;
As sister and brother,
And there is nothing better
Than when we are together.

'Twas love that brought us together,
And love is keeping us together
So we will be together
Forever and ever.

Love brought us together,
And love is holding us together,
And there is nothing better
Than when we are together.

S G Grizzle

FIRST LOVE

Broken dreams, a broken heart,
Since the day we've been apart.
A tear-stained pillow, from tear-filled eyes.
All because we've said goodbye.
We could have made it, but we never tried.
And too many friends told too many lies.
They stole our rainbow, they hid the sun,
They spoilt the love that had just begun.
So now you're gone, I walk alone.
A lonely heart without a home.
But if you're lost too, just look for me,
And we'll walk hand in hand to eternity.

Sue Allison

LOVING SOMEONE

Your hands are gentle,
Wrapping my hair in your fingers,
Your fingernails tickle my spine,
But bite into the palms of your hand,
When you clench your fist.

Your sculptured eyebrows rise in delight at me,
But can corrugate up in silent anger.
Your eyes sparkle teasingly,
But can close in frustration and pain.

Your mouth
Lingeringly soft,
Teases mine,
Can twist provokingly
Spitting daggers in my defiant face.

You wonder,
I think.
Two stars locked in the dark,
I'm an enigma you're trying to work out.

We've survived through the pain and tears,
What the world has thrown at us,
We've caught,
And thrown back.

We're best friends,
Partners in crime.
You're my universe.

Lorna Goodall

TRUE LOVE

I was only fourteen and still a young girl,
When suddenly you set my heart in a whirl,
'This has to stop' my Mother said,
But I let my heart overrule my head,
'Engaged at sixteen you're far too young,
You should be going out having fun,'
I told her then you were the one for me,
And two years later she had to agree,
At St Nicholas' church I became your bride,
On September the first as we stood side by side,
We had two children to complete our dream,
By now we were proving quite a team,
We've now been married thirty three years,
And our love grows stronger as retirement nears,
I have never regretted becoming your wife,
And my love is yours till the end of my life.

Celia Law

MY VALENTINE

V's a voice that thrills me through
A's for ankles neat and trim,
L's for legs so long and slim and
E's for eyes of clear, clear blue.
N's a neck, smooth and down soft,
T's for teeth which gleam so white.
I's for instep high and light.
N's a nose that tips aloft, while
E's the everlasting love I'll feel for you throughout my life.

V's a voice that slurs each word,
A's for ankles tree trunk style,
L's for lips that twitch not smile.
E's for eyes that now are blurred,
N's the neck like wrinkled prune
T's for teeth not now your own,
I's the instep flat foot grown,
N's the nose with constant rheum and
E's an everlasting love that sees you still as young and fair,
   my dearest wife.

Daisy Thomson

NEW LOVE

Love you forever and forever,
For now you are endearing.
As I send my love to you,
Be awake,
As I am gleaning,
Your grinding,
Screening,
Waiting for the day you really love,
So I can say,
Whatever.

Vicky Robinson

PERENNIAL

Our love is like a precious bulb,
Planted in the warm autumn soil,
Replete with promise of perfection.

Deep in the ground it grows,
Stretching out, tentatively drawing
From the earth's nourishing womb.

With the onset of winter, icy fingers
Plunge into the soil, intent on destruction.
They chill, but do not kill us.

And, as the weak, pale sun regains its throne,
We unfurl ourselves towards its majesty,
And burst through deepest darkness into light.

Parading Easter bonnets of glorious hues,
Exuding joy and perfumed incense,
Consummating our promise.

Yet, summer soon advances,
Bowing our backs, withering our leaves,
Forcing retreat to our earthy home.

Down we go, into the blessed soil,
Content, for death is but a hibernation,
Before a brilliant, new dawn.

Karen Costello-McFeat

UNTIL YOU CAME ALONG

There had been a dream somewhere
That had never been spoken -
A wild wish hushed
Never unveiled.

There had been a hope somewhere
That others would have mocked -
A masked ambition
Hidden from the world.

There had been a secret somewhere
Lurking like the hunted -
A strange obsession
Kept to myself.

Dreams, wishes, hopes
Ambitions, secrets, obsessions -
Covered up and laughed off
Until you came along.

Camilla Romaine

REGRET

The song you asked me to sing
Remains unsung to this day.
I have spent time
Day after day
Night after night
Knitting my words with joy and delight
Unknitting them with anger and pain.
The words are only words.
They are not true to you,
There is in my heart
This agony to be true to you
Which wrenches me apart.
My best beloved, only now
I know who filled my eyes with tears
And my person with sunshine.
I will wait for you, waiting on you,
Playing my games with you.
Till I become true and behold you, my most dear.

Angela Cutrale Matheson

WHISPER

You whisper gently in my ear
Those lovely words I long to hear
To feel your cheek so close to mine
It wakes the flutter deep down inside

My heart it always skips a beat
And makes me flustered each time we meet
I long to feel your gently touch
That makes me feel alive at heart

And when you hold me oh so tight
I wish you might stay all the night
I want to feel your body close
To be as one with you the most.

Amanda Small

UNREQUITED LOVE

Oh, my love, my love.
You never once looked on my face
Except to see the friend there,
You rest your head on my shoulder
Only to cry there,
Your tears of misery
When your love of you was unaware.
And I in my dark despair
See you now with your love, so fair.
Happy for you I should be
But how can I tear myself free
From the chains of love that bind me
In deep bands of misery.

Susan Ogden

SUCH SWEET SORROW

And though I know deep inside my heart,
That for a while we must be apart.
Every moment that I spend away,
Fills up a lifetime in just one day.

My heart is like the petal of a delicate flower,
That lies in your hands and gives you the power,
To make my days full of sunshine or my heart full of rain,
To fill me with joy or crush me with pain.

I thirst for your touch - find peace in your arms,
I long for your kiss - will succumb to your charms.
Yet you've hurt me in places I didn't know could feel,
And shown me the anguish of a love that is real.

I hold to your promise that soon this will end,
That given time and your love my broken heart will mend.
That this separation will be but a terror of the night,
And together we'll share a future that's bright.

Victoria L Williams

A SINGLE RED ROSE

A rose so delicate
So pretty so unique
A rose with qualities
A gift so petite.

But what joy that rose
So small can produce
A sign of love and happiness
Which I give to you.

Marie-Louise Bate (14)

HEARTACHE

How shall I say I love you
When you don't heed the words that I say
How can I prove I love you
In some convincing way
How must I say I love you
When words don't express what I feel
How many times must I repeat it
To convince you that it is real
Shall I tell you of the feeling
That deep down responds to your name
Of the glow that I feel when I hear it
That suffuses the whole of my frame
I love you my dear for without you
My world will crumble and die
And to think of the future without you
Brings many a tear to my eye
What more can I say to assure you
That my love for you is steady and strong
And if you'd feel the same way about me
Then nothing could e're break our bond.

Hubert Hayes

EN FLAGRANT DELIT

I cannot pretend to have
Forgotten, though I suppose
The time has come to let go.
As we walked, hand in hand
All over now, another wave
Hitting the fragile shore.
Nothing, if it isn't there
Any more is worth remembering.

I see your face as if on a
Fast moving train, but
Travelling in the opposite
Direction am I, pressed against
Sound proof glass, every memory
Sharp flashbacks reflected from
Millions of tiny mirrors.

Then I see myself forming a smile
Until tears break into ripples in
My mind's eye;
I saw you with her once too often.
Falling backwards, losing love
Down a thorny ravine
That is just life you said but
Some things are simply unpardonable.

My fate in love seems to have
Already have been decided
My eyes see in black and white, colours
Fade, walking away from my sight.
Erased though you are from my
Answering machine tape.

By ending it all by telephone
You committed a terrible faux-pas
En flagrant delit, in flagrante delictus
Caught in the act, you worthless narcissist,
You have finally grown feral, you may as well
Have stabbed me in the heart!

Each day I awake to a smiling sea of sky
An ocean I see and breathe but like you
Cannot feel, just resigned to
Drown in the distant vision,
Slowly reliving the day your gaze
Turned away from mine, to settle on another
But I realise now,
Though it took some time
That she deserves you better.

Linda Louisa Evans

WEDDING ANNIVERSARY

These passing years are simple walls
Masked by the tapestry our hands
Have made and hung there;
Bright testament to love which calls
As strongly through this air
Of autumn, as in the distant lands
When spring had unseen artistry
Making perfection in each scene.
The years have made us free
Of all this treasure which has been
Our trust for us to hold, to show
For all other lovers as they go
By this way: it will be their own
As it is ours. No lovers go alone.

Eric Chapman

LOVE LETTERS

I will keep holding on,
Never to let you go,
All you want will be done,
Because I will never say no,
I must keep the tightest grip,
Or else you'll drift away,
My fingers will never slip,
I want you every day,
All I need is you here,
I'm complete when you're close,
Losing you is my worst fear,
Your the one I want the most,
Love letters in ink or lead,
And all of the perfumes around,
Flowers of white, pink and red,
Your feet won't touch the ground,
If we were ever to split or part,
I'd like you as a close friend,
Although a new romance would start
Our love should never end.

Chris Fletcher

HEARTBREAK

Another day, mist surrounds her,
Trapping - it's closing her in
As the day progresses, it gets worse
She's caught, no escape.

He is unaware
Feelings crushed into oblivion
An impossibility
She wonders what 'she's like'
He is out of reach,

Under a spell,
Secretly, subconsciously he knows it too
Her secret,
Kept pressed to her heart -
She longed for a heart of stone.

Tears of passion and lust
Are lost.
Held now is too much regret,
Selfish thoughts invade,
But reality and intelligence
Re-lights her
Once again.

The wind rushes around,
The frost crisp in the air,
The crack of ice underneath
As she waves him goodbye
He turns to walk away . . .

Linnet Allison

LOVE

Butterfly kisses
Lips like wine,
Eyes with love so bright
Love so wonderful
In candle light
Towering feeling
So so true.
My love for you
Thoughts night and day.
Only powerful for you
Just you.
Why do I find life's worthwhile
Simply because,
I own your wonderful smile,
So my darling
It's got to be,
For life - forever
Just you and me.

M Chapman

YORKSHIREMAN

He's sixty now, but vigorous and hale,
White-haired, with a complexion fair and pale,
Ice-blue short-sighted eyes still clear and striking -
Legacy perhaps of some ancestral Viking;
Big crooked teeth in an engaging grin,
High craggy brow, smooth-shaven cheeks and chin.

Fine singing voice, tenor or baritone,
Distinctive speech, especially on the phone;
Long arms; neat nails on big-veined shapely hands,
Something above the middle height he stands.

He is a star, and I his greatest fan,
This gentle, strong, beloved Yorkshireman.

Helen Parsons

MY VALENTINE

Was it love at first sight? No sir
No way in my life that did occur
In fact in my life when young I was so shy
To tell you different would be telling a lie
Oh what did I miss? Yes folk I just sigh
Then out of the blue my luck had changed you see
Someone was interested in little me
At a factory where we both did work
Always busy no time to no way shirk
What happened next I was asking this girl for
A date to which she did refuse would not ask no more
But to my surprise the next day this lass said yes
Was I happy yes like a dog wagging a tail I guess

She was a Yorkshire lass - from Sheffield yes
I asked her to marry who? yes me
To look after her do my very best
She was the idle of my young life was she
We have been married 57 years going on for 58
Her name is May my love my life that's great
My May I loved her when we were young still do
We have a very nice family all grown up now that's true
After all the years gone by our love has got stronger
Fifty seven years let's hope it will go on longer
My loving wife will always be my valentine
I loved her then when we first met and all the time
The best wife a man could ever have my May
Suits me just fine that I will yes folk do say
God look after us both of that I do yes pray
On February 14th again I name her my true
Love on this Valentine's Day -

Just Tom (Sexton)

LOST LOVE

A great lake looms
Time which must be crossed
I know it is hopeless
And I will fail
What else can I do?
Keep swimming
I cannot drown either.

I feel nothing
A numbness
Smothering and complete
Standing at the window
Perhaps for hours
Looking for a signal
Something physical
A long run
The answer's always
so much stronger

What for?
I won't go crazy with this
Simply dead.

Moira Thorburn

ODE TO ROMANCE

Like some planets have rings,
There's an aura about you
As the dawn's early light
Throws a silver dust mist-dew
While you dance in bare feet
Amongst lilac and heather
If your love had wings,
I would fly you forever.

As the stars say goodnight,
Your presence grows brighter
Whilst you waft around honey-suckle,
Sweet as pure nectar
Your laughter infectiously,
Spreads like the weather
If your love had wings,
I would fly you forever.

Now the sun comes to greet you,
With the gold of the morning
As you stand silhouetted,
Against the day's new dawning
Inviting such passions
That will bring us together
If your love had wings,
I would fly you forever.

Michael Gardner

REMEMBER

The things I remember
When our love was so tender

The cool breeze through the nights
The rain drops fall like sparkling lights

November leaves fall
To the ground
When I come to call
You're never around

I miss your love
And only wish
That you'll remember
My love and my kiss.

Aisha Romilly

FORBIDDEN LOVE

In secret they met
With love in their eyes
And time spent with friends
This love to disguise:
The touch of a lip
The brush of a hand
A moonlit walk along the sand.

A separation
Hearts grow dear
A time apart
And all is clear:
A love to last and trust and live
Willing hearts to take and give
Lovers' memories, lovers' smiles
And truest love
True lovers' child.

Deborah Fitz-Gibbon

I WAIT NO MORE

For love I waited
For the soft whisper of the man who bears the other half of me, I
waited.

For friendship pure and true - I waited
I stood broken heart heaving in my chest, awaiting
Standing silent, praying that his heart will one day love me
Desperately, I waited
Tense, exasperated
Emotions well castrated.

For simple thanks, for good deeds done - I waited
Long, lonely winter nights
the hail stones beating on my window pane
The cold wind blowing on my soul, I waited.

Others should also bear the pain of waiting
their hearts a beating in their chests,
the urgency,
the treacherous blows dealt out by fate for waiting

A slave to time and fate I'll no more be
I've had my earthly share of desperately awaiting
I wait no more,
For it is *I* who now shall be awaited.

Georgina Laverse

SUMMER LOVING

I
Sneeze
Love
Sneeze
You
Sneeze

I mumbled into
My handkerchief
As we skip
(well I stumble)
Through long grasses.

Michael Leeman

EMOTION CONFLICT

Love's many faceted illuminae,
Changing night to light and
dark to day.

Spiralling euphoria
plunging down, turning
bittersweet heartsong
smile to frown.

Close your eyes and
you will see,
Unbidden thoughts
of destiny,
Of where you
will meet and
love and hold,
Entrusting
your secrets
to keep safe
and hold.

These fragile emotions
as brittle as glass,
Twisting and turning
just out of your grasp.

How quickly they shatter,
imploding your heart,
With cuts cold as steel
and sharp as Hell's wrath.

See love's words melt,
Under cold light of morn,
and float away like the mist
that dissipates with the dawn.

Maureen Braithwaite

THE RAVES

All at once,
Like passing judgement
Your love absence
Not knowing what the grudge meant

I'm sorry Debbie
For I never knew
That a love for me
Was growing inside of you
I hope and I pray
We'll be back together some day
Until then
There'll be other women

Then the memory fades
As we touch the blades
Of the Jack of Knaves
One night stands for me and raves.

Mirko Vukasinovic

MY BELOVED

His love is more fragrant than any perfume,
My beloved for me is a cluster of the finest pearls,
How beautiful is my dearest.
He is like a mighty oak amongst thousands of thistles,
To sit in his shadow is my delight,
For on a hot day his shadow is cool.

Have you seen of whom I speak?

He is a wall, his shoulders are towers,
They were created to protect and defend me.
His body is a fermented spiced wine,
And his hair is of a flowing raven black.
His whispers are sweetness and light
And his hands are strong, yet gentle when they caress.
His legs are like columns of marble
And his arms are gold satin to enwrap me.

It is my true love to you I describe.

When he returns we will lie on the camomile lawn,
And delight in the garden picking roses of red.
My heart is sinking when he is not here.
He did not steal my love for I gave to him freely.
I am awaiting to give him all my love
Which is even mightier than death
And blazes up like a fierce fire.
He is the thirst in me that cannot be quenched
How my heart aches for his return.
Come to me, I am waiting,
Oh, my dearest, my darling, my beloved.

Rita Hazelden

WORDS

Words are insufficient
To tell you how I feel;
Too clumsy, inappropriate,
Mundane, and yet unreal.

Words cannot hope to capture
This fire within my soul,
Nor hope to paint a picture
That in any way is whole.

Words fail to reach the centre
Of a feeling that's so pure,
And cannot probe such depths of love,
So, need I utter more?

Vikki Silverlock

WINE AND ROSES

When the night around me falls
I think of you and I recall
Our days of wine and roses
I hear your voice and see you smile
And then for just a little while
I think of wine and roses
Our days of love I live again
You come to me a while and then
Before I fall asleep to dream
I think of wine and roses
I loved you then I love you now
I still recall our sacred vow
So until I see your smiling face
And hold you in a fond embrace
I'll live my life in dreams of you
And our days of wine and roses

Barbara Scriven

CONFUSED

Have you ever felt so confused
That you just want to leave this world behind?
Find another place and time

How do we know what's the best thing to do?
How can we ever choose
When there could be so much to lose
Not least my happiness

How did it all begin?
Life becomes a blur
People are staring, I realise I'm crying
Please, can't somebody help me?

Whatever happens, someone will be hurt
Could it be me?

Maybe neither way is the truth
I thought my life had found its course
What caused this change in my thoughts?
Or did anything change?

It's too late now to stop the wheel
Time to go with the flow
Maybe no-one will know

Perhaps fate is lending a hand
It is the right move
Because I love you

I'm sure.

Victoria Lillie

MY REGRETS

You came along with a smile for everyone.
You shared your laughter, and your chocolate,
and you always smelt of home baked bread.
I remember when you met my mum.
You moved in.
I resented that. I resented your presence;
your laughter, that smile
But they never went away.
You fought for my affection.
But I refused to acknowledge you.
You made everybody laugh while I sulked and missed out.
You never backed down. You hurt when I hurt,
You cried when I cried.
I spent all those years wishing you'd go away
and now you have, and I miss you.
I know it's too late, but I realise now,
Just what you had, and what you gave,
and that smile.
How hard you tried to make me love you.
And I know I never said it,
but, for what it means,
I love you.

Lucy Jude

PEED SI EVOL

What is love? I ask myself,
When you are left, on the shelf,
If ignored by one you fancy,
You tend to feel, a proper nancy.

When you, are on your own,
And sit by a silent phone,
All your friends, are out clubbing,
In deep despair, you are blubbing.

Dark and draughty little room,
Filled with anxiety and gloom,
Lay on your bed, gaze at the ceiling,
No one knows, just how you're feeling.

But that was when I was seventeen,
Zits on face, I felt obscene,
Now I am in my later years,
I no longer have those fears.

There have been many girls in my life,
Once, even took a wife,
Eventually, when that was over,
Life is full, and I am in clover.

So you lads, do not worry,
To go with girls, there is no hurry,
I really know things get better,
She will find you, so go and get her.

Robert Thompson

LIQUID, AGAIN

The butter upon your lips
The blood within your veins
The sweat that pours from your smooth dark brow
Like scented summer rains.

Such is the life I lead
Warmed by your love's bright flame
Held close to your heart till I find that I too
Am returning to liquid, again.

Elizabeth Gallagher

SLEEPLESS NIGHTS

There came a great quiet as our lips met
A disembodiment of the world - a soaring into space
That was at once silent yet
Filled with strange wonder more awesome
Than any beauty that I ever beheld.
All the stern efforts not to think of my troubles -
Not to let the memories come
Stealing in to fill my sleepless nights.
Missing you with an unrelenting, penetrating hunger.
The hour of revelation locked deeply in my heart -
Only in the hopeless depths of despair did I
Resort to the memories of lying in your arms
Knowing the meaning of love - of belonging.
Love is knowing when to let go.

Eileen Clifford

BEING WITH YOU

The thing that I miss most about you is,
The smell of your scent,

The touch of your hair
The thought of a feeling that won't disappear
Heaven would be,
Being with you under an umbrella without any rain.
Holding hot chocolate just after a hurricane.
Understanding a mime and being able to make your
Songs Rhyme.
Being with you is like finding a penny every day.
Being with you, is like a good film with a
Disney end.
In the end, being with you
Will do.

Dave Williams

TO ASK HER WHY?

Last night, while we were walking,
She took my arm.
And looped hers around it.
It was an unusually warm feeling -
At once, I was at peace with myself.

But. I don't know why she did it.
Was it love?
Or maybe, a fear of being alone
In the dark.
Perhaps it was just friendship.
If I only knew.
I would have asked,
I would,
But my friend came by.
And so to she - I had to say
'Bye'
Before I had chance
To ask her why?

George Thomson

LOVE ALL AROUND

Flowers are blooming
Grass is green
Wind is sweet.
Every living thing is growing
It's heard and seen
From the speed of heartbeat.

Sun is shining low,
Together with
Moon and the stars
Clouds with a rainbow
Apparent and vivid
As gems in a glass.

Sky in an embrace
With the earth
Elements go hand in hand
Forgetting to race
Creating a sign of rebirth
In every nation and land.

S Alam

THE LETTER

You know I have always loved you
from your first baby cry
to this present day

I have always tried to help
from the first day of school
till your first day at work

Have you ever realised
how each problem was solved
and each tear dried away
It was easy because I loved you

Now you have gone from me
I have given you away
and someone else will dry those tears
and care for you

But I know you will still come to me
with a problem or two
because you are my daughter
and you know I care.

Maureen Lord

WHAT IS LOVE?

If love is the sun then let me shine
On all things down below
If love is a grape let me be the wine
To be drunk so sure and slow

If love is an ocean let me try
To swim through waves so strong
If love is an eagle let me fly
'Til the light of day has gone

If love is the grass then let me grow
Far through the soft brown earth
If love is wisdom let me know
The depth of its true worth

If love is a letter then let me write
The words so sweet and true
If love is a battle let me fight
To always be loved by you.

Anne Wheble

ONE TYPE OF LOVE

I want to go where the sun don't shine
To where the rivers run bone dry
To where the trees refuse to bloom
And the air is filled with gloom

I want the darkness to surround me
To touch my very heart
To join my soul in sadness
And hold my pain in madness

I want to run into a never ending night
To where your presence shines so bright
To where your memory lives on and on
Never to be gone never to be gone

I want to embrace you with a hug
To hold you forever and ever
In this never ending night
Where we never need see the light - again.

Debbie Avery

LOVE IS . . .

Love is . . .
dreaming of the lad in question.

Love is . . .
often mistook for indigestion.

Love is . . .
when you feel strangely sick.

Love is . . .
responsible for making us tick.

Love is . . .
found in the heart and the head.

Love is . . .
reading too much into anything said.

Love is . . .
a dominated soul and mind.

Love is . . .
often hard to find.

Love is . . .
luckily, sometimes reciprocated.

Love is . . .
eagerly anticipated.

Love is . . . ?

Pamela Sibbering

INFORMATION

We hope you have enjoyed reading this book - and that you will continue to enjoy it in the coming years.

If you like reading and writing poetry drop us a line, or give us a call, and we'll send you a free information pack.

Write to :-

**Arrival Press Information
1-2 Wainman Road
Woodston
Peterborough
PE2 7BU**